Gluten Free Alchemy:

The *Heart & Soul*

of Creating
Gluten Free Goodies

Written & Photographed by
Joan Bender, MA, LMHC, HC

That which the fire operates is alchemy,
whether in the kitchen or in the universe

- Paracelsus 1493-1541

To contact the author, visit
www.jbenderwellness.com

Printed by CreateSpace, An Amazon.com Company

ISBN-10: 0-692-94424-9
ISBN-13: 978-0-692-94424-0

Printed in the United States of America

DEDICATION

This book is dedicated to all who express themselves and show their love through the creation of delicious foods.

We are all Alchemists

You don't have to be a chef or even a particularly good cook to experience proper kitchen alchemy: the moment when ingredients combine to form something more than the sum of their parts.

-Erin Morgenstern

Acknowledgements

A special heartfelt thank you to all of you who believe in me and cheer me on. I also want to acknowledge and thank those who helped with the production of this work.

Thank you to my friends, Ruth Ann and Jennifer, for your proof reading and feedback, and for being brave enough to sample my treat experiments.

Thank you to my friend, Rogean, for your formatting expertise and artistic eye.

Thank you to my husband, Ken, who bravely tastes my treats, gives me excellent advice, makes me laugh at myself and encourages me to keep trying.

Thank you to my dog, Grace, who eats all of my mess ups and thinks that they are the best treats in the world.

Thank you to my sisters, Jean and Elizabeth, who supported me emotionally, helped to test some recipes and cheered me on all along the way.

Thank you to my childhood friend, Phyllis, for all of our fun times playing in the kitchen and experimenting with food.

Thank you to Magi and Janine for always encouraging my big leaps.

And a big thank you to my Mom, Grandmother, Aunt Tillie in heaven and my Aunt Joan, cousins, Kim and Kris, and my friend Ellie for showing me the value of cooking and baking with whole foods and demonstrating how to express love through the sharing of food.

And finally, a big thank you to my chickens who supply me with beautiful eggs for all of my cooking and baking experiments.

A special thank you to the Kickstarter backers who helped to make this cookbook possible.

Clint Williams
Marissa Gandelman
Catherine Baxter
Gina Lee
Thomas Vincent
Jennifer Wick
Janine Murphy
Sebastian Lange
Sandy Wickenheiser
Etta Fink
Denise Jordan
Lisa Chorost
Robin Shafer
Jean Hagin
Ellen Lattrell
Jean DelPorte
Boom Kat
Noreen Gill
Bill Gettman
Lynette Mazzuca
Bree Decker
Koppany Otto
Amanda Neaton
Krissy Birchard
Ruth Ann Smalley
Ben H.
Red Herring Games LTD
Danielle Baker

DISCLAIMER

This cookbook is a product of Joan Bender, Health Coach and Food & Mood Coaching LLC and is a compilation of recipes that the author has developed and enjoyed since eliminating gluten over 10 years ago. Food sensitivities can be complicated and this book is not intended to be a substitute for conventional medical treatment. It is suggested that you continue to work with qualified medical professionals as you engage in our material, products and services. Please refrain from using any ingredients that you might be sensitive to in any way. Information and statements provided in this book regarding products and/or services made available by Joan Bender, Health Coach, have not been evaluated by the Food and Drug Administration. The Author comes from the school of thought that healthy is different for everyone. The terms "healthy" and "healthier" used in this book are in comparing these recipes to average store bought, highly processed, baked goods that are high in sugar content and low in nutritional density. Information, products and services of Joan Bender, Health Coach and Food & Mood Coaching LLC are not intended to diagnose, treat, cure or prevent any disease. This book is the intellectual property of Joan Bender, Health Coach and Food & Mood Coaching LLC and cannot be modified, copied, reproduced, republished, uploaded, posted, transmitted, translated, sold, exploited or distributed in any way without written consent and citing its source.

Elixir of Life   27
Buckwheat Crepes   29
Traditional Crepes   29
Cinnamon Apple Pancakes   31
Blueberry Cacao Pancakes   33
Berry Pancake Sauce   33
Banana Bread & Muffins   35
Banana Bread French Toast   35
Lemon Berry Muffins   37
Blueberry Banana Flax Muffin   39
Carrot Muffins   41
Mascarpone Cheese Frosting   41

Breakfast Cookies   43
Raw Gingerbread   45
Chocolate Orange Tea Treats   47
Lemon Ginger Tea Treats   47
Coconut Lime Tea Treats   49
Nut & Dairy Free Tea Treats   49
Cinnamon Chocolate Cherry
Cookies   51
Oatmeal Cookies   53
Egg Replacer   53
Hazelnut Cookies   55
Traditional Gingerbread   57
Hungarian Honey Hearts   59
Pumpkin Bars   61
Lemon Blueberry Coffee Cake   63

Peanut Butter Brownies   65
Raspberry Cream Brownies   67
Cinnamon Apple Cake   69
Chocolate Nut Torte   71
Chocolate Frosting   71
Chocolate Pudding Cake   75
Chocolate Pudding   77
Frozen Bonbons   79
Cashew Cream   83
Apple Pecan Pie   85
Banana Tea   87
European Style Dumplings   89
Stuffing   91

More than a cookbook: A return to that which is pure & good

Do you eat to live or do you live to eat? For me, it's both. I eat for nutrients to fuel my body, build tissue and create strong muscles and bones, but I also eat to feed my soul with colorful, delicious, flavorful foods. What and how we eat makes a difference, and I believe that we are being called to connect with food in a different way. Not a new way, though it may be new to some, but in an older, more primal way. You see, as a whole, we have lost our sacred connection to food and where it comes from. We've lost touch with understanding how food feels in the body. We have also been convinced that things like acid reflux, bloating, and other digestive distress is a normal symptom of aging or overeating, and that we can take a pill to feel better, when most often those pills further disrupt our digestive processes. We debate about whether there is something wrong with the body, or the food, or the chemicals that are being used on and in our food, with little resolve, and leave those with food sensitivities feeling deprived and less whole. The reality is that our bodies are screaming out for pure, clean foods, with vibrant sun-kissed colors that not only feed our cells, but also our souls.

In addition, we eat with our thoughts on other things, and we leave the table feeling unsatisfied and wanting more, because we haven't taken the time to prepare, smell, witness or taste our food and feel it settle into our bellies. We've turned over the growing, harvesting and preparing of our food to factories and the cooking of it to microwave ovens. In doing so, we have lost a connection to the cycle of life, the reciprocity of giving to our food and our food giving back to us, and the sense of fulfillment that comes from creating beautiful, colorful, nutritious and delicious foods that feed, nourish and bring joy to our friends and family. All of this has influenced the quality of the food that we eat and our bodies are calling out to us to make some changes.

Cooking and baking for oneself is the ultimate form of self-care and self-love. There is a very real physical and medical component to our food sensitivity, but I believe that there is also a spiritual component that gets overlooked by our western medicine philosophy. I believe that component is self-love. We get so busy in life caring for others and putting the priorities of others above ourselves. The reality is, we need to care for ourselves first before we can care for others. When the body starts falling apart, it is calling us to return to caring for ourselves. Healthy is different for everyone and not everyone is made to eat wheat or gluten. Our food industry has told us that it is an important part of our health and much of our medical industry has accepted this. However, we can live very happy and healthy lives without it, when we are ready to start listening to our bodies over all of the external noise. It is my hope that this cookbook will serve as more than a book of recipes, but also a guide to connecting with your food in a different way.

Joan

We all have a complex web of food & mood memories

We all have a complex web of food experiences that started before we were born, continued to develop through infancy, childhood, and continues to change and develop to this day. Do you have fond memories of cooking or baking as a child, or watching your mom or grandmother as they cook or bake? Do you remember the smell of the foods wafting through the air, and the anticipation of tasting those delicious treats? I certainly do. Growing up I was surrounded by women who loved to bake. These women expressed their love for their friends and families through the creation of delicious treats. I can remember helping my mom even at a very young age. One of my favorite things to do was grind nuts for her chocolate nut torte (p.71). She had an old-fashioned grinder; the kind where you had to crank the handle to manually grind the nuts. She insisted that the nuts were ground more finely this way, creating a fluffier cake. Her nut torte with butter cream frosting was my favorite dessert. My mom actually let me eat this cake for breakfast, when I was a kid. She said that it had more protein than boxed cereal, and she was right. Luckily, when I started eating gluten free, I could still eat this cake, because it doesn't contain any gluten.

Saying good-bye to favorite foods is one of the toughest transitions for people with food reactions. I did have to say good-bye to some of my favorites like crepes, honey cookies and the chocolate pudding graham cracker cake with whipped cream, but only temporarily. As time went on, I began experimenting. My sister and cousin both have celiac disease, and by the time I stopped eating gluten, our family had already begun the transformation into gluten free alchemy.

The unexpected happened

In the beginning, I felt like I had given up so many delicious foods, and I can remember saying, "I will never give up sugar and sweets. I have already given up enough!" Sound familiar? However, as time went on and as I started eating healthier and making my own baked goods, I started feeling like many of the recipes I had been using were way too sweet. I started cutting back on the amount of sugar in recipes and started experimenting with alternative natural sweeteners. The result of this was feeling more energetic, having less highs and lows and less cravings.

Your transformation has begun

Where are you in your gluten free transformation? Going gluten free involves an internal and external transformation. Some people are able to make the external transformation but inside, they long for foods from the past and maintain a feeling of deprivation. Things may taste different or have a different texture, but they can still be delicious. I reached a point in my healing journey where I not only wanted yummy sweet treats, but I wanted to feel good after eating them. I no longer wanted the ups and downs, the brain fog, and the lightheadedness of eating sweet treats. I started to slowly cut back on sugar. Then I started experimenting with alternative sweeteners.

Connect with Your Food in a Different Way

Where are your thoughts when you cook and bake? Are they on your to-do list, tomorrow's activities, self-criticisms of the day, the loss of eating your favorite gluten filled foods, how you don't have time to cook or that you now have this curse of a food sensitivity or autoimmune disorder? It is time to make a mindful shift, and bring different thoughts to your experience. Believe it or not, this has an impact on the taste quality of your food. Like you, most days I am in a rush and my thoughts are all over the place. I feel like I need to quickly throw ingredients together and move on to the next thing on the to-do list. However, over the last few years, I've found myself connecting to food in a different way. I find myself admiring the beauty of it, appreciating it, loving it up and admiring the intelligent relationship between our bodies and food.

As you gather your ingredients, take a moment to really look at them. Think about where they came from. Think for a moment about how there is life in that nut, seed or berry. Think about the time it takes to fully ripen. Think about how it can be planted to grow a tree or plant that bears more food. Think about how it has nutrients in it that your body can use to fuel your brain, build tissue, and give your hair, skin and nails a healthy glow. You don't have to spend a lot of time thinking of these things, just make a quick recognition of the beauty and magic of it all. When I do this, I not only feel more present and connected to my food, I also find myself feeling a sense of gratitude.

Alchemy & Stocking Your Gluten Free Pantry:
Choose only the best ingredients.

We are fortunate to have many types of gluten free flour and products on the market these days. At first, I was annoyed about using multiple types of flour in one recipe, but now I love the diversity. Exposing ourselves to a variety of flour types exposes us to a variety of nutrients and flavors that we wouldn't be having if we were still eating wheat.

This list is based on the recipes in this book, a guide to knowing what you'll need to create these treats. I'm not paid to endorse any brands, but I do specify those that I use based on quality preference. Using a different brand might change the taste or texture of the recipe especially when gluten free flour is concerned. You'll see that I use a variety of gluten free flours and sweeteners that are low Glycemic. This helps us to feel more "even" physically and emotionally, and decreases the chances of having a sugar high and crash. This way, you can give your soul some sweet treats while going easy on your body.

Nut Flours- Nut flours are full of fiber, healthy fats, protein and are lower in carbohydrates. This makes them a lower Glycemic alternative to wheat and rice flour. By stocking your pantry with raw, unsalted nuts, you can make your own nut flour by grinding nuts in a food processor. It doesn't take long and is more economical. When your nuts are ground at the time of baking, they will be more flavorful and fresh tasting. If you grind more than you use, store them in a glass jar to maintain their flavor. Storing them in the refrigerator helps to maintain freshness as well. Don't store them in plastic containers. The oil from the nuts breaks down the oil in the plastic and it leaches into the food. This creates a plastic taste and brings toxins into your food. Almonds and hazelnuts create a drier texture, while walnuts create a very moist texture. Pecan flour is less dry than almond and hazelnut, but not as moist as walnut. Enjoy experimenting with these to find your favorites.

Flax meal- Flax meal is high in fiber and omega-3 oils. It adds moisture to your baked goods, and it also absorbs excess moisture, giving your baked goods a nice texture. You can also buy whole flax seeds and grind them when needed. This will help ensure their freshness.

Coconut flour- Coconut flour is higher in protein and fiber, and lower in carbohydrates, so it has a lower Glycemic index than rice flour. It adds a mild coconut flavor to baked goods. It is very economical, because you need only a small amount in most recipes. If you want to experiment with some of your favorite recipes, the conversion is approximately 1/4-1/3 cup coconut flour to 1 cup of other gluten free flours.

Buckwheat flour-Don't be fooled by the name. Buckwheat is not a form of wheat, and it is gluten free. It isn't a very pretty flour, in my opinion. It creates dark grey baked goods and has a coarse texture, so I like to blend it with other gluten free flours. It is high in fiber and protein, low carbohydrate and creates baked goods that are lower on the Glycemic index. It is also a good source of magnesium, calcium, amino acids, iron and copper. It is nice for breakfast pastries, cereals and pancakes, because it is filling and satisfying.

Sorghum flour- Sorghum is an ancient grass. Its seed is used for cereal and ground into flour. It is high in fiber and protein and its starch is digested slowly, which makes it low Glycemic. It is a good source of vitamins B, E, and K as well as the minerals magnesium, selenium, phosphorus, zinc, iron and copper.

Oat flour- Oat flour is a good source of B vitamins, but it is lower in protein and higher in carbohydrates than buckwheat, sorghum, and nut flours. You can make your own gluten free oat flour by grinding gluten free oats in a food processor or other food grinder. Gluten free oats have been grown and processed in dedicated areas where they aren't cross contaminated with other grains like wheat. Make sure the oats you buy are labeled gluten free.

Arrowroot powder- Arrowroot is a starch that comes from the rhizomes of several tropical plants. It is a good thickening and gelling agent. Using arrowroot to thicken can sometimes be tricky. When using arrowroot as a thickening agent in puddings, gravies and sauces, add it to cool liquid to dissolve and get lumps out before adding to hot liquid. Simmer on a medium heat. Once the mixture has thickened, remove it from heat. Leaving it on the heat for too long will cause the mixture to thin again. Arrowroot can also be added to homemade ice creams to prevent ice crystals from forming so that your ice cream has a more workable texture. When using as a substitute for corn starch, you can substitute as an equal measurement.

Organic corn starch- Most corn starch on the market today is made from genetically modified corn. Many people who have a wheat sensitivity also have a sensitivity to corn. I've found that organic corn feels fine in my body, however non-organic corn creates problems like gut and joint pain. If you are staying away from corn products, you can switch out arrowroot powder or tapioca starch for corn starch as an equal measurement.

King Arthur gluten free flour blend- This is my favorite flour blend. I like it best, because it feels best in my body. It is a blend of rice, potato and tapioca. This blend is higher Glycemic than nut flours, so I often mix it with a higher protein nut flour, buckwheat, or sorghum flour.

Storage

Store ingredients, especially nuts and oils, in glass containers.

When stored in plastic containers, the oils from the plastic leach into and bind with the oils of the ingredients. This has an effect on the taste of the ingredients as well as contaminates your food with hormone-disrupting toxins from the plastic.

Baking Soda (Sodium Bicarbonate)- is a leavening agent that causes a dough or batter to rise when it is mixed with something acidic like lemon or honey. Once it combines with the liquid it begins acting, so it is usually combined with other non-liquid ingredients, first before adding to the liquid ingredients.

Aluminum-Free Baking Powder- There are three types of baking powder. Fast-acting begins working with liquid ingredients, slow-acting contains aluminum and begins acting when the aluminum becomes hot in the oven, and double-acting is a combination of fast-acting and slow acting baking powders. I prefer to use the fast-acting aluminum-free baking powder to avoid consuming aluminum.

Xanthan Gum & Guar Gum- These are thickeners and emulsifiers. They help to keep baked goods together. They can have a little bit of an aftertaste, so I use them minimally.

Oils:
Grapeseed oil vs Coconut oil- Both grapeseed and coconut oil are great dairy-free alternatives for baking. I prefer grapeseed oil for baking when I want to use a non-dairy fat, because it has a very mild flavor and incorporates well into baked goods. Coconut oil will add a coconut flavor to your baked goods, and sometimes feels a little greasy. Grapeseed oil has a higher smoke point than coconut oil, therefore it is better for cooking and baking at higher temperatures.

Avocado Oil- I don't use avocado oil much, but it is a healthy oil for cooking and baking, and has a high smoke point.

Why I don't use vegetable oil or canola oil: Vegetable oil is usually made from corn or soybean both of which have become genetically modified. Canola oil is made from rapeseed, a part of the brassica family of plants, and has also been genetically modified. These oils have been processed in a way that uses high heat, chemicals and solvents process them.

When comparing different oil brands in the store, look for the words expeller pressed and cold pressed on your oil labels.

Essential Oils and Organic Fruits and Vegetables- I try to use organic fruits and vegetables in my baking, especially if I am using the zest of citrus fruits. Make sure you wash them well. Many people don't realize it, but organic doesn't mean that the produce is spray free. It just means that if sprays were used, they must be organic approved sprays. I recently started using Young Living brand essential oils in some of my baked goods, because they are pure and shelf stable. They end up being more economical, yet they maintain their integrity. Young Living has a seed to seal process that ensures the oil's purity and authenticity. You can learn more about Young Living's Seed to Seal Process by going to www.youngliving.com.

Natural Sweeteners:
Honey- When possible, use raw, local honey especially in the raw recipes. Raw honey is alkaline and contains antioxidants, phytonutrients and enzymes that are lost when it is processed. There is a safety precaution: Do not feed raw honey to children under age one.

Nektar crystals- Nektar is a brand of honey crystals that resemble sugar, but are made from honey. Sometimes I use this as a sweetener when I want to add a little sweetness, but don't want to add more a liquid to the recipe.

Maple Syrup- Use only pure maple syrup. That means that maple syrup is the only ingredient. Some brands add corn syrup, colors and flavorings. You'll want to stay away from those. Grade A is harvested earlier in the season and is lighter in color and has milder maple taste. Grade B is harvested later in the season and has a darker color and stronger maple taste.

Stevia- This sweetener comes from the stevia plant. It has a sweeter taste than sugar, but doesn't raise blood sugar. Some brands mix stevia with other sweeteners like dextrose, sucrose and xylitol, so read ingredient labels carefully. I use the Sweetleaf brand. It should be noted that some people who have an allergic reaction to chrysanthemum, marigold, ragweed and daisies might also be allergic to the stevia plant. I am one of those people who is allergic to ragweed, but stevia doesn't seem to bother me. If you have allergies, proceed with caution and consult your health care provider before experimenting.

Raw Coconut Nectar- Comes from the trunk of the coconut tree just like maple syrup comes from the truck of the maple tree. This sweetener is low Glycemic, low in fructose and contains 17 amino acids plus other vitamins and minerals. This sweetener can usually be swapped 1:1 with sugar and other sweeteners.

Guideline for Baking with liquid sweeteners: The general rule for baking with liquid sweeteners is to decrease a dominant liquid in the recipe by about 2 tablespoons per each ½ cup of liquid sweetener. The modifications for the recipes in this book have already been made, but if you decide to experiment with making substitutes in your favorite recipes, you might have to play around a little bit to get things to your liking.

Why I don't use agave. I am often asked about agave as a natural sweetener. I don't use it for several reasons. It is a low Glycemic sweetener, however it is processed in a similar way to high fructose corn syrup, so it is high in fructose which makes it hard on the pancreas and gets converted to fat by the liver. I also seem to have an allergic reaction to the agave plant and I get horrible migraine headaches following eating anything made from agave. I have met others who have this same reaction. I have also found it to have an addictive quality. When I've eaten things made with agave, I can't stop. I keep eating more and more.

There are many more sweeteners to play around with like date sugar, coconut sugar, birch syrup just to name a few. Each has their own unique flavor and benefits, so when you're feeling brave, try experimenting with them.

Organic/ free-range/ grass- fed eggs and dairy products- When possible use organic, free-range eggs and dairy products from organically raised grass-fed cattle and free range chicken. In my opinion, these animals create a better product, because they are eating a more diverse diet than commercially raised animals.

Dried fruits that have no added sugar or are sweetened with fruit juice- Store dried fruits in glass jars to maintain their freshness. Like nuts, when they are stored in plastic, they will pick up the taste of the plastic and bring toxins into your food.

Natural dyes and sprinkles made from natural dyes- You can find these in most grocery stores and health food stores. I have included a couple of brands that I use on the on-line resource page at the back of the book.

Bleach and dye-free cupcake wrappers- When possible, I prefer to use bleach and dye-free wrappers, so as to prevent chemicals from leaching into my baked goods. One time I made the lemon berry muffins and put them in red, Valentine's Day cupcake wrappers only to have red-dyed muffins.

Raw cacao- Cacao beans are turned into chocolate. When the beans are roasted at very low temperatures to maintain their antioxidants, they are called raw cacao. I like using raw cacao in the uncooked recipes to maximize my antioxidant intake.

Allergen-free chocolate chips- Enjoy Life brand has dairy-free, soy-free, nut-free, gluten-free chocolate chips.

Decorate with edible berries, flowers, and herbs- You can use pansies, hibiscus, chicory, mint leaves, pomegranate seeds and fruit slices in place of sugary sprinkles when decorating baked goods.

My Measurements:

Many of my mother's recipes were measured with handfuls, pinches and dashes. Some of those measurements have been carried into these recipes. Enjoy the freedom of making your handfuls, pinches and dashes as big or little as your heart desires.

Handful- I usually use this measurement for chips, nuts, and dried fruit. Reach in and grab a handful. Stir it into the recipe. Look it and decide if you are happy with the proportion. If you want more, add more.

Pinch- I usually use this measurement for salt. I pour a little in the palm of my hand and then grab a small amount with the thumb and pointer of my other hand. That's my pinch.

Dash- I usually use this measurement for spices that are in a sprinkle type container like cinnamon. Just tip over quick and let some fall out.

Sprinkle- A sprinkle is four-to-five dashes.

Transforming gluten free ingredients into delicious and nutritious treats that not only feed our cells, but also our souls-- That's gluten free alchemy.
— Joan Bender

ELIXIR OF LIFE

Elixir of Life

Ingredients:
¼ cup grated beet
¼ cup grated carrot
1 tablespoon raw sunflower seeds
½ cup raspberries
1 banana
Handful of greens (kale, beet greens, Swiss chard, spinach)
1-2 tablespoons almond butter or protein powder
Non-dairy milk (Coconut, almond, cashew, rice, hemp)

Grate one small beet and one small-to-medium carrot and put in a high speed blender container. Add some raw sunflower seeds, raspberries, banana & greens. Add enough milk to cover the ingredients in the container. You can also add some almond butter or high quality protein powder. Put it in the blender, Ninja, Vitamix, Nutribullet or what have you, and blend on high speed until you've got a smooth, creamy texture.

Voila! You've created a beautiful, delicious smoothie.

Yields: 1 serving.

Get That Golden Glow

You can't have a cookbook called Gluten Free Alchemy, without having an "Elixir of Life."

This smoothie recipe is packed with a vast array of enzymes, vitamins, minerals, antioxidants and phytonutrients to nourish the body, mind and spirit.

It makes a quick, easy healthy breakfast or mid-day snack. If you need more than a smoothie for breakfast, add in one of the muffins or breakfast cookies.

BUCKWHEAT CREPES WITH
BERRIES & CASHEW CREAM

Buckwheat Crepes

Ingredients:
¼ cup sweet white sorghum flour
¼ cup buckwheat flour
3 eggs
1 teaspoon vanilla
1 tablespoon flax meal or ground flax seeds
3 tablespoons of milk (almond, rice, and coconut, dairy)
Coconut oil or organic butter for greasing the pan

Traditional Crepes

Ingredients:
¼ cup plus 1 tablespoon sweet white sorghum flour
¼ cup organic cornstarch or ¼ arrowroot powder
2 tablespoons flax meal
2 eggs
½ cup organic milk
½ teaspoon vanilla
½ tablespoon melted organic butter (you'll also need butter for greasing the pan)

Combine ingredients and whisk until all of the lumps are worked out. Your batter should be a little thinner than pancake batter. If it appears to be too thin, stir in a ½ tablespoon more flax meal and let it rest for a minute. Flax meal thickens as it absorbs liquid. If it starts to thicken too much as it sits, add a few drops of milk and stir well. Melt a pat of butter in a pan over medium heat, and add a ladle full of crepe batter. Tilt and turn the pan so that the batter spreads thinly over the surface. When the edges begin to crisp and the liquid has become solid, give the crepe a flip to brown the second side. This is the fun part. It is all in the wrist. Give that crepe a toss in the air and catch it back in the pan!

Yields: 4-5 crepes depending on the size of the pan.

Crepes made with buckwheat are heavy and hardy while traditional crepes have a lighter feel. Both are packed with protein.

Alchemy Tips:
The trick to making beautiful looking crepes is to wipe the pan with a paper towel after each crepe is cooked and removed from the pan. Then melt a new pat of butter before adding new batter. This keeps the butter from getting too brown and burning.

Filling: Spread Greek yogurt, nut butter or fresh fruit on your crepes. Then roll them up and dig in.

CINNAMON APPLE PANCAKES

Cinnamon Apple Pancakes

Nut free recipe
Ingredients:
¾ cup brown rice flour
½ cup tapioca flour
¾ cup milk
1 teaspoon vanilla
1 egg
1-2 apples- peeled and sliced thin
Sprinkle cinnamon to taste

Almond Flour Recipe
Ingredients:
¾ cup brown rice flour
½ cup almond flour
1 egg
¾ cup milk
1 teaspoon vanilla
1-2 apples peeled and cut into small slices
Sprinkle cinnamon to taste

Combine the flour ingredients and cinnamon in a bowl. Add the eggs, vanilla and milk. Whisk until well blended and lumps are worked out. The batter should be thin, but not watery. Finally, stir in apple slices. If too thick, add a few drops liquid. If too thin add a little flour.

Melt butter or heat oil in a pan on medium to medium low heat. Add a ladle full of pancake batter. When edges start to crisp, flip over and cook the second side. The pancakes are cooked when both sides are browned and cooked through the middle.

A Classic

These were my favorite pancakes growing up and remain so today.

They are made without baking soda so they have a heavier, denser consistency than our American style pancakes.

Alchemy Tips:
If you use coconut oil to cook these, leave your heat on low-to-medium low so you don't burn the coconut oil. There's not much worse than burnt coconut oil.

Yields: approximately 8-10 three-four inch round pancakes.

My preferred fat for cooking pancakes is sea salted butter, but if you need to eat dairy-free, I suggest grapeseed or coconut oil to grease your pan.

BLUEBERRY CACAO PANCAKES

Blueberry Buckwheat Cacao Pancakes

I like to top these with Greek yogurt, berry sauce, or peanut butter.

Ingredients:
½ cup brown rice flour
¼ cup buckwheat flour
¼ cup tapioca flour
¼ teaspoon baking powder
1 large egg
½ cup, plus 2 tablespoons, milk of your choice
2 dashes cinnamon
2 tablespoons raw cacao
1 tablespoon maple syrup or 1-2 packets Sweet Leaf stevia
½ cup fresh blueberries
Handful of mini chocolate chips (optional)
Butter or oil for cooking

Combine flour, cinnamon, baking powder and cocoa in a mixing bowl. If using a powder stevia like Sweet Leaf instead of maple syrup, add it to your flour mixture. Add your liquid ingredients to your dry ingredients. Whisk until all lumps are gone and then fold in blueberries and chocolate chips.

Melt butter or heat oil in a pan on medium to medium low heat. Add a ladle full of pancake batter. When edges start to crisp, flip over and cook the second side. The pancakes are cooked when both sides are browned and cooked through the middle.

Yields: approximately 8-10 three-four inch round pancakes.

Berry Pancake Syrup:

Instead of pouring syrup on your pancakes, make a nutrient dense berry sauce by simmering a cup of berries, ½ cup of water and a tablespoon of pure maple syrup. Cover & simmer on low heat until the fruit simmers into a sauce.

Alchemy Tips: If you use coconut oil to cook these, leave your heat on low-medium low so you don't burn the coconut oil. There's not much worse than burnt coconut oil. **Blah!**

BANANA BREAD FRENCH TOAST

Banana Bread and Muffins

Ingredients:
1 ripe banana
3 large eggs
¼ cup grapeseed oil
½ cup coconut flour
1 tablespoon flax meal
1 tablespoon vanilla extract
½ teaspoon baking soda
½ teaspoon baking powder
Handful of chocolate chips
Handful of chopped walnuts
Dash of cinnamon

In a mixing bowl, mash the banana. Add all of the wet ingredients and stir or beat until they are mixed well. Stir in the dry ingredients until they are well incorporated. Fold in the chips and nuts. Pour into a muffin or bread pan and follow baking instructions in the sidebar.
Yields: about 6 muffins or 1 loaf of bread.

Banana Bread French Toast

To make banana bread French toast, all you'll need is slices of the banana bread above and 1 large egg for every 1-2 slices of banana bread. Crack the eggs in a bowl, add 2 tablespoons milk and beat with a fork. Add the banana bread, one slice at a time and coat each side of the bread with egg. Heat a skillet with a pat of butter or tablespoon of oil and place the egg-coated bread slices in the pan. Cook on medium to medium-low heat until each side is lightly browned and cooked through.

Go Bananas

To make muffins: Pour into greased or paper lined muffin pans and bake at 350° for 25-29 minutes.

To make bread: Double the recipe above and pour into a well greased 8 ½ x 4 ½ x 2 ½ pan. Bake at 350° for 45-50 minutes or until inserted toothpick comes out clean.

Alchemy Tips: Coconut flour is very absorbent and you need only a small amount, usually a ½ cup coconut flour to 3-4 eggs.

LEMON BERRY MUFFINS

Lemon Berry Muffins

Double for 12 muffins

Ingredients:
3 large eggs
½ tablespoon flax meal or 1 tablespoon chia seeds
½ cup coconut flour
¼ teaspoon baking soda
¼ teaspoon aluminum free baking powder
¼ cup grapeseed oil
8-10 drops lemon essential oil*
½ tablespoon water
½ cup chopped fresh berries
½ teaspoon vanilla extract
¼ cup pure maple syrup, honey, or coconut nectar
Dash of cinnamon
Handful of mini chocolate chips (optional)

Combine the liquid ingredients and the dry ingredients in separate bowls, then add the dry ingredients to the liquid ingredients and mix on low speed or by hand with a whisk. Fold in berries and mini chips last. Spoon batter into a greased or paper-lined muffin pan.

I like to sprinkle a little cinnamon on top and top with a couple of berries.

Bake at 350° for 20-25 minutes.
Cool on a rack.

Yields: 6 muffins.

So Many Possibilities

I've tried these muffins with all kinds of berries, but my two favorites are raspberry and cranberry.

Alchemy Tip:
*The lemon essential oil can be replaced with fresh lemon juice and lemon zest. Use ½ tablespoon juice of a lemon and a ½ teaspoon lemon zest.

BLUEBERRY BANANA FLAX
MUFFINS

Blueberry Banana Flax Muffins

Ingredients:
½ cup ground pecans
½ cup flax meal
½ cup oat flour
½ cup dry oats
½ teaspoon baking soda
½ teaspoon baking powder
¼ cup chopped walnuts
2 large eggs
¼ cup grapeseed oil
1 ripe banana, mashed
½ cup frozen wild blueberries

Combine dry ingredients in a mixing bowl. Add oil and eggs and stir until well combined. Gently stir in blueberries last. Spoon the batter into greased or paper-lined muffin pans.

Bake at 350° for approximately 20-25 minutes. Check doneness with a toothpick. Muffins are done when tops are slightly golden brown and tooth pick comes out clean.
Cool on a rack.

Yields: about 8 muffins.

Golden Flax Seeds

Contain healthy omega-3 oils that nourish your skin, hair, nails, heart, and brain.

Alchemy Tip:
You can buy already ground flax meal or make your own by grinding golden flax seeds in a spice or coffee grinder.

Don't throw away your banana peels. You can make them into a delicious tea. See page 91.

CARROT CAKE MUFFINS

Carrot Cake Muffins

Ingredients:
1 cup ground walnuts
½ cup oat flour
1 cup dry oats
½ cup pure maple syrup or honey
2 eggs
¼ cup grapeseed oil
½ teaspoon baking soda
½ tablespoon vanilla extract
½ tablespoon cinnamon
½ teaspoon nutmeg
1 cup shredded carrots (1-2 large carrots)
Handful mini-chocolate chips or raisins (optional)
Grind the walnuts in a food processor or blender. Put all of the dry ingredients in a mixing bowl, then add the liquid ingredients and stir well. Finally add the carrots and optional mini-chocolate chips or raisins. Bake in the oven at 350° for 20-25 minutes.
Cool on a baking rack.
Yields: 6-8 muffins.

Mascarpone Cheese Frosting

I prefer this topping over cream cheese frosting.

Ingredients:
8 oz. mascarpone cheese
1 tablespoon vanilla extract
2-3 tablespoons maple syrup or honey

Do you juice?

Alchemy Tips:
Did you know that you can use the pulp to create delicious muffins?

Just replace the cup of carrots in the carrot muffin recipe with a cup of juicer pulp.

Here are some great combinations to try:

Carrot, beet, orange

Apple, carrot

Carrot, orange, cranberry

Combine the ingredients in a bowl and stir until well incorporated. Spread on cooled cupcakes.

BREAKFAST COOKIES

Breakfast Cookies

Ingredients:
¼ cup raw cashew unsalted pieces
¼ cup almond flour
¾ cup unsweetened shredded coconut
4-5 dried pitted dates
¼ cup dried cherries
Dark chocolate chips
1 teaspoon vanilla extract
2 large eggs

You can make these cookies two ways. You can make a no bake/raw version or a baked version.

No Bake Version:
Leave out the eggs from the recipe. Put all of the other ingredients in a food processor with a cutting blade and combine until all of the ingredients are chopped and dough is a sticky consistency. Roll into balls or shape into bars.

Bake version:
Put cashews, dates, cherries and chocolate chips in a food processor and pulse until nuts and dried fruits are ground. Stir in the rest of the dry ingredients and then add the eggs and vanilla and stir well. Drop spoonfuls onto parchment paper lined cookie sheet. Bake at 350° for 8-10 minutes. Let cool and then enjoy!

Yields: about 15-20 spoon-sized cookies.

Yes! You can have cookies for breakfast!

Alchemy Tips:
If you are making the no-bake version and are having a hard time getting them to form into balls, you can stir in a tablespoon coconut oil, nut butter or sunflower butter to help hold things together.

These raw cookies and tea treats pair nicely with a cup of Tulsi tea. Tulsi is an Indian herb that is adaptogenic, so it adapts to what the body needs.

RAW GINGERBREAD COOKIES

Raw Gingerbread Cookies

Ingredients:
1 cup raw unsalted cashews
½ cup sliced almonds
½ cup chopped pecans
14-16 pitted dates
1 teaspoon vanilla extract
2 teaspoon ginger powder, or slice of ginger root grated (about 1 inch thick)
½ teaspoon allspice
Sprinkle of cinnamon
½ teaspoon nutmeg
¼ cup dark chocolate shavings or mini chocolate chips

Combine all ingredients except chocolate in a food processor (cutting blade) or grinder. Pulse grind until dough becomes sticky. Stir in chocolate. Form dough into balls or other cookie shapes and chill for at least 1 hour.

Yields: about 18-20 cookies.

Try me with a cup of hibiscus tea.

For a traditional Gingerbread recipe, see page 57.

Go Raw

Alchemy Tips:
If your dough is too dry and doesn't form a ball, here are some things you can do.
You can pulse the ingredients in the food processor. This will help to release more of the natural sugars and oils.

I also find squeezing the dough in my hands first helps things to stick together before rolling it into balls.

You can also stir in a spoonful of coconut oil or nut butter to help hold things together.

CHOCOLATE ORANGE TEA TREATS

Chocolate Orange Tea Treats

Cookie Ingredients:
1 cup almond flour
1 cup ground cashews
1 tablespoon flax meal
14-16 dried pitted dates
12-14 drops orange essential oil
1 teaspoon vanilla extract
1 handful mini chocolate chips

Coating Ingredients:
1 tablespoon raw cacao
1 tablespoon organic powdered sugar
Dash of cinnamon

First, combine the vanilla and essential oils. Next, put all of the cookie ingredients except chocolate in a food processor with chopping blade or grinder. Pulse grind until dough becomes sticky. Stir in chocolate. Form dough into balls. In a small bowl combine raw cacao, cinnamon and powdered sugar. Roll the balls around in the coating and chill for at least 1 hour. **Yields**: about 18-20 cookies.

Lemon Ginger Tea Treats

1 cup almond flour
1 cup ground cashews
1 tablespoon flax meal
14-16 dried dates
1 slice of ginger root (about ½ inch thick)
1 teaspoon vanilla extract
1 handful mini chocolate chips
12-14 drops lemon essential oil (or 1 teaspoon lemon zest & 1 teaspoon lemon juice)
Follow directions above, including rolling in the chocolate coating.

Time for Tea

Tea time is a time to slow down, pull back and appreciate our surroundings.
-Letitia Baldridge

Tea Treat Alchemy Tips:
Follow the tips for Raw Gingerbread on the previous page.

For a **nut & dairy free** version of Chocolate Orange Tea Treats, see page 49.

*If you don't have orange essential oil, use 1 teaspoon juice of an orange and 1 teaspoon

COCONUT LIME TEA TREATS

Coconut Lime Tea Treats

Ingredients:
1 cup almond flour
1 cup ground cashews
1 tablespoon flax meal
14-16 dried dates
12-14 drops lime essential oil (or 1 teaspoon lime zest & 1 teaspoon lime juice)
1 teaspoon vanilla extract
1 cup shredded coconut (1/4 cup to incorporate, the rest to roll the balls in)

First combine the vanilla and essential oils. Next, combine all of the ingredients in a food processor with a chopping blade or grinder. Use only ¼ cup of the coconut in the recipe and put the remainder in a bowl. Pulse grind until dough becomes sticky. Form dough into balls, roll in the shredded coconut, and chill for at least 1 hour.
Yields: about 18-20 cookies.

Get Energized

You'll be surprised at how satisfying, filling and energizing these tea treats are. They are small, but nutrient dense. They not only go well with tea, but they complement the Elixir of Life for an energizing way to start your day.

Alchemy Tips:
Follow the tips for Raw Gingerbread on the page 45.

Nut & Dairy Free Tea Treats for Susanne

Ingredients:
1 ½ cups gluten free dry quick oats
1 cup sunbutter
¼ cup ground flax seeds or flax meal
3-4 tablespoons non-dairy milk or 1 additional tablespoon sunbutter*
Sprinkle of cinnamon
2 handfuls of mini dairy-free chocolate chips
1 teaspoon vanilla
12-14 drops orange essential oil (optional)
Combine ingredients and mix well. Roll into small balls and roll in the chocolate coating from the Chocolate Orange Tea Treats recipe on the page 47.*If your sunbutter isn't already sweetened, you might like to add 2-3 tablespoons maple syrup or honey.

CINNAMON CHOCOLATE CHERRY COOKIES

Cinnamon Chocolate Cherry Cookies

Ingredients:
4 tablespoons organic butter
10 oz bag of dark chocolate chips
1 tablespoon raw cacao or
unsweetened cocoa powder
2 large eggs
½ cup brown sugar or coconut palm
sugar
¼ cup +2 tablespoons almond flour or
oat flour
2 teaspoons cinnamon
1 teaspoon vanilla
½ cup dried tart cherries
½ cup chopped pecans

Pre-heat oven to 350°. Combine chocolate chips, butter and unsweetened cocoa in a double boiler and stir until butter and chips melt. You can create a double boiler by putting water in a pot and then putting another pot on top. Put the ingredients in the top pot. The boiling water in the lower pot will melt the chocolate and help to prevent burning.

In a mixing bowl, beat eggs, vanilla and sugar for 2-3 minutes. Add the flour and chocolate mixture and beat on low until combined. Fold in cherries and pecans. Chill in refrigerator for 15 minutes. Drop spoonfuls onto a parchment paper-lined cookie sheet. Bake 10-12 minutes. Cool on a rack.
Yields: 18-20.

Ken's Favorite

Alchemy Tips: This dough spreads quickly on the cookie sheet. Also, watch closely while they are baking, especially your first batch, because they can burn easily.

Dairy Free Version: To make this recipe dairy-free, you can replace the butter with coconut oil and use dairy-free chocolate chips
.

OATMEAL COOKIES

Oatmeal Cookies

Ingredients:
¼ cup almond flour
¼ cup gluten free oat flour
¼ cup coconut flour
2 teaspoons cinnamon
½ teaspoon baking soda
1/8 teaspoon salt
1-2 packets stevia
1 ½ cups gluten free rolled oats
½ cup plus 1 tablespoon brown sugar, maple sugar or coconut palm sugar
1 ½ teaspoons vanilla extract
2 large eggs
¼ cup melted organic butter or grape seed oil
½ cup dark chocolate chips (optional)
¼ cup chopped walnuts or pecans (optional)
¼ cup dried cranberries, cherries, raisin (optional)

Combine dry ingredients in a mixing bowl. Add eggs, vanilla and oil. Stir until well blended. Fold in optional items last. Place spoonfuls on cookie sheet pan, and bake at 350° for about 10 minutes or until golden. Let cool before removing from pan.

Yields: about 2 dozen cookies.

Egg Replacer

Alchemy Tips:
Are you sensitive to eggs? Try this Bob's Red Mill recipe as an egg replacer.

Combine 1 tablespoon flax meal to 3 tablespoons water and let sit for 5 minutes. Then add to the recipe as you would add an egg. Recipe equals 1 egg. Double for 2 eggs, triple for 3 eggs, etc.

(Reprinted with permission from Bob's Red Mill.)

HAZELNUT COOKIES

Hazelnut Cookies

Ingredients:
2 cups hazelnuts
¾ cup sugar or coconut palm sugar
4 large egg whites
½ teaspoon salt
1 teaspoon vanilla extract
1 teaspoon cinnamon
Dark chocolate shavings

Put the nuts and sugar in the food processor until finely ground.
Separate the eggs, putting the whites in a large mixing bowl. Beat the egg whites, vanilla and salt until they form stiff peaks. Gently fold in nuts, sugar, chocolate shavings and cinnamon.

Line a cookie sheet with parchment paper. Place spoonfuls of the dough onto cookie sheet and bake at 350° for 25-30 minutes. For best baking results, see the Alchemy Notes in the side bar. Let cool before removing from pan.

Yields: about 20-24 cookies.

Don't throw out those egg yolks:
You can add them to omelets or your morning oatmeal for extra protein. You can brush the bottom crust of a pie to keep the crust from getting soggy, add to the pudding recipe on page 77 to make custard, make a lemon curd or crème brûlée. You can also freeze them to use at another time.

Crispy & Nutty

Alchemy Tip:
Make sure the oven rack is in the middle of the oven.

These cookies burn easily when the rack is too low and close to the heat source.

You may need to adjust the cooking time based on your oven, so watch the first batch carefully.

GINGERBREAD COOKIES

Traditional Gingerbread Cookies

Ingredients:
1 stick organic butter
1 egg
½ cup brown sugar or coconut palm sugar
1/3 cup molasses
1 cup sorghum flour
1 cup almond flour
½ teaspoon salt
1 teaspoon aluminum free baking powder
2 teaspoons guar gum or 1 teaspoon xanthan gum
1 teaspoon ginger
½ teaspoon allspice
1 teaspoon cinnamon
1 teaspoon vanilla extract

Preheat oven to 350°. In a mixing bowl, combine softened butter, brown sugar, molasses, egg and vanilla. When mixed well, add the dry ingredients and blend on low speed. Form the dough into 2-3 balls. You can flour your hands with some sorghum flour and sprinkle some sorghum flour on top of the dough pile to keep the dough from sticking to your hands. Wrap each dough ball in wax paper or BPA free plastic wrap and chill in the refrigerator for a couple of hours. Once the dough has become firm, remove from the refrigerator (and wrapper) and place on a sorghum-floured cutting board and roll with a rolling pin to your desired thickness. Cut out shapes with cookie cutters and place the cookies on a parchment paper-lined baking sheet. Decorate with sprinkles or chocolate chips.
Bake at 350° for about 10-12 minutes. See sidebar.

Holiday Favorite

Alchemy Tips:
If the dough sticks to the rolling pin, you can dust more flour onto the pin and the dough.

You can also put a piece of wax paper between the dough and the pin.

Baking time will vary based on your oven and the thickness of your cookies.

HUNGARIAN HONEY HEARTS

Hungarian Honey Hearts

Ingredients:
½ stick unsalted butter
½ cup brown sugar or coconut palm sugar
1 cup honey
1 ½ cups King Arthur Gluten Free Flour blend
1 cup sorghum flour
½ teaspoon baking soda
1 egg
1 tablespoon cinnamon
2 tablespoons raw cacao
Pinch of salt

Preheat oven to 350°. In a mixing bowl, combine softened butter, brown sugar, honey, egg and vanilla. When mixed well, add the dry ingredients and blend on low speed. Divide the dough into 2 or 3 piles and form each into a ball. You can flour your hands and sprinkle some flour on top of the dough to keep it from sticking to your hands. Wrap the dough in wax paper or BPA free plastic wrap and chill in the refrigerator for a couple of hours. Once the dough has become firm, remove from the refrigerator (and wrapper) and place on a floured cutting board. Roll with a floured rolling pin to your desired thickness. Cut out shapes with cookie cutters, and place the cookies on a parchment paper lined baking sheet.

Bake at 350° for 10-12 minutes. Once the cookies have cooled, you can melt dark chocolate in a double boiler on low heat and dunk the cookies into the chocolate or drizzle melted chocolate over the cookies with a spoon. Set on a wax paper-lined cookie sheet until chocolate sets and hardens.

Spread the LOVE

Alchemy Tips:
If the dough sticks to the rolling pin, you can dust more flour onto the pin and the dough.

You can also put a piece of wax paper between the dough and the pin.

Baking time will vary based on your oven and the thickness of your cookies.

PUMPKIN BARS

Pumpkin Bars

Ingredients:
1 cup almond flour
½ cup coconut flour
2 tablespoon ground flax seeds
½ teaspoon baking soda
2 tablespoons brown sugar or coconut palm sugar
2 teaspoons cinnamon*
½ teaspoon nutmeg*
3 eggs
1 cup plus 2 tablespoons puree pumpkin
¼ cup honey**
2 tablespoons grape seed oil
Handful of dark chocolate chips

Instructions:
Preheat oven to 350°. Combine the dry ingredients. Then add eggs, pumpkin, honey and oil. Stir until well combined. Stir in the chocolate chips last.

Pour into greased 8x8 pan.

Bake at 350° for 25-30 minutes.

Let cool for at least 20 minutes. Slice into bars and enjoy!

Fall Favorite

Alchemy Tips:
*You can add more or less of the spices according to your taste preferences.

**This recipe is low on the sweetness scale. If you want to make them sweeter, but want to keep the Glycemic index down, you can add 1 packet of Sweetleaf stevia or another spoonful of coconut palm sugar.

LEMON BLUEBERRY COFFEE CAKE

Lemon Blueberry Coffee Cake

Ingredients:
5 drops lemon oil (or 1 teaspoon lemon zest & 1 teaspoon juice of a lemon)
1¾ cups almond flour
½ cup honey
2 large eggs
½ teaspoon baking soda
½ teaspoon baking powder
Pinch of sea salt
2 tablespoons grapeseed oil
4 oz mascarpone cheese
1 tablespoon maple syrup
1½ tablespoons vanilla (1 tablespoon for the cake batter and ½ for the cheese topping)
½ cup blueberries
Sprinkle of cinnamon and chopped pecans

Preheat oven to 350°. Combine mascarpone cheese, ½ tablespoon vanilla and maple syrup in a bowl and set aside. In a mixing bowl, beat the eggs, vanilla, lemon, salt, grapeseed oil and honey for one minute on low speed. Add almond flour and beat again on low speed for another minute. Pour batter into greased 8x8 baking pan. Add small spoonfuls of mascarpone cheese mixture and gently swirl into the batter. Top with blueberries, pecans and cinnamon. If you like things sweet, you can sprinkle a little brown sugar on top.

To make a dairy free version:
Omit the mascarpone cheese.

Alchemy Tips:
When baked and hot, the top edges will be browned but the middle will be jiggly and look unbaked. This is due to the mascarpone cheese being melted.

Once the cake cools and sets, it will become firm.

Bake at 350° for 28-30 minutes. Once out of the oven, let the cake sit on a rack to cool. Once the cake has cooled and settled, it will be firm, and is ready to be sliced and eaten.

PEANUT BUTTER BROWNIES

Peanut Butter Brownies

Ingredients:
1 cup chocolate chips melted
3 eggs
¼ cup grapeseed oil
1 cup almond flour
2 tablespoons coconut flour
2 tablespoons raw cacao powder
½ tablespoon vanilla extract
½ cup brown sugar or coconut palm sugar
½ cup cooked, mashed sweet potato (optional)
2-3 tablespoons peanut butter

Melt the chocolate chips in a double boiler. Combine ingredients in a bowl until well incorporated. Pour into an 8x8 greased pan. Add a couple of spoonfuls of peanut butter on top and gently swirl through with a fork. Bake about 20-25 minutes at 350°.

Kick this recipe up a healthy notch and add ½ cup cooked mashed sweet potato. You'll add fiber, phytonutrients, while the sweet potato also adds moistness.

Cure That Craving

Alchemy Tips: You can make this recipe with or without the sweet potato. The sweet potato adds moistness as well as fiber & nutrients.

Don't have raw cacao? You can use an unsweetened cocoa powder like Hershey's.

No one has ever guessed that there is sweet potato in these brownies.

Add a little salty, smoky, savory kick and crumble up a few slices of cooked crispy bacon and sprinkle it in. I prefer to use an all natural, uncured bacon that is nitrate or nitrite free, or contains only naturally occurring nitrates and nitrites.

RASPBERRY CREAM BROWNIES

Gooey Fudgy Raspberry Cream Brownies

Brownie Ingredients:
1 cup chocolate chips melted
3 eggs
¼ cup grapeseed oil
1 cup almond flour
2 tablespoons coconut flour
2 tablespoons raw cocao powder*
½ tablespoon vanilla extract
½ cup brown sugar

Cream Topping Ingredients:
8 oz. mascarpone cheese
1 tablespoon vanilla extract
2 tablespoons maple syrup or honey
½ cup fresh or frozen raspberries

Preheat oven to 350°. Melt the chocolate chips in a double boiler. Combine all of the brownie ingredients in a bowl until well incorporated. In a separate bowl, combine all of the topping ingredients except the raspberries until well-mixed. Pour the brownie ingredients into an 8x8 greased pan. Drop spoonfuls of the cream topping on top and gently swirl into the brownies. Finally, sprinkle the raspberries on top.

Bake at 350° for about 20-25 minutes.

Gooey Goodness

Alchemy Tips:
When these brownies are warm, they are a gooey consistency. When they are chilled, they are similar to a fudge consistency.

*Don't have raw cacao?
You can use an unsweetened cocoa powder like Hershey's.

CINNAMON APPLE CAKE

Cinnamon Apple Cake

Ingredients:
2 cups almond flour
¼ cup flax meal
5 large eggs
¼ cup grapeseed oil
1 teaspoon vanilla
½ teaspoon aluminum-free baking powder
½ teaspoon baking soda
½ teaspoon nutmeg
½ teaspoon allspice
2 teaspoons cinnamon
1/3 cup honey
3 medium-sized apples

Preheat oven to 350°. Cut the apples into small thin slices and set aside. In a mixing bowl, combine the wet ingredients and beat slightly with a whisk, or on low speed with an electric mixer. Add in almond flour, flax meal, spices, baking soda and powder. Beat again on low speed until ingredients are well-combined. Fold in the apple slices and pour into a greased cake pan (small bundt or 8x8 square pan). Bake at 350° for about 30-35 minutes or test with a toothpick. It is done when the toothpick comes out clean.

Ah! The smell of cinnamon...

Alchemy Tips: This treat is low on the sweetness scale. If you decide you like this sweeter, you can add a couple tablespoons of honey or a packet of stevia.

If you want to put frosting on this cake, the mascarpone frosting on page 41 pairs nicely.

CHOCOLATE NUT TORTE

Mom's Chocolate Nut Torte

Ingredients:
10 eggs separated
10 tablespoons sugar
¼ cup cocoa powder
3 ½ cups ground nuts (equal amounts ground almonds & walnuts)
1 teaspoon vanilla extract
2 teaspoons aluminum free baking powder
4 semi-sweet Hersey's chocolate bar baking squares- grated

Preheat oven to 350°. In a large mixing bowl, combine cocoa, ground nuts, baking powder and grated chocolate. Separate the eggs into 2 separate bowls, one with whites and one with yolks). Add 6 tablespoons sugar and vanilla to the egg yolks and beat with an electric mixer until thick. Add 4 tablespoons of sugar to the egg whites and beat until very stiff peaks form. Gently fold together the yolk mixture and the egg white mixture. Then fold in the nut mixture. Pour into greased bundt or spring form pan. Bake for at 350° for 30-35 minutes. Take out of the oven and let sit for a few minutes. Then place cooling rack on top of cake pan and flip over. As the cake cools, it will release from the pan.

Traditional Version

Alchemy Tips:

Test doneness with a tooth pick. The tooth pick will come out clean when the cake is fully baked.

Frosting: Once fully cooled, frost with the butter cream frosting below or with the non-dairy coconut cream frosting on page 76.

Mom's Frosting is not low Glycemic. See page 73 for low Glycemic versions.

Mom's Chocolate Butter Cream Frosting
1/3 of a 1lb box organic confectioner's sugar
2 sticks of unsalted butter, softened
¼ cup Hersey's unsweetened cocoa
1 teaspoon rum or black coffee (optional)
Beat ingredients on low to medium speed, until smooth and creamy.

CHOCOLATE NUT TORTE CUPCAKE
WITH COCONUT CREAM &
POMEGRANATE

My Easier Version of Mom's Chocolate Nut Torte

Ingredients:
3 cups whole walnuts or pecans
½ cup honey
¼ cup cacao or cocoa powder
½ cup dark or semi-sweet chocolate chips
1 teaspoon aluminum-free baking powder
¼ teaspoon baking soda
1 teaspoon vanilla extract
10 eggs

Preheat oven to 350°. Put all of the ingredients in a food processor or vitamix (minus the eggshells, of course). Pulse until the nuts are ground and you have a smooth batter. Pour into greased cake pan. Bake at 350° for about 35 minutes or 18-20 minutes for cupcakes. Test with a toothpick. When it comes out clean, the cake is finished baking. Take out of the oven and let sit for a few minutes. Then, place cooling rack on top of cake pan and flip over. As the cake cools, it will release from the pan. Once fully cooled, frost with chocolate butter cream frosting, non-dairy chocolate coconut cream recipe on page 79 or chocolate avocado frosting in the side bar.

My Chocolate Butter Cream Frosting
¼ cup maple syrup
2 sticks of unsalted butter
¼ cup raw cacao or Hersey's unsweetened cocoa
1 teaspoon vanilla extract
3 tablespoons arrowroot powder

Beat ingredients on low to medium speed until smooth and creamy.

Quick & Easy

Who has time to grind nuts and separate eggs? Try my quick and easy version of Mom's Nut Torte.

Alchemy Tips:
Do you love avocado? Try this non-dairy frosting. Mix the flesh of 2 avocados with, 4-6 tablespoons cacao, 6 tablespoons maple syrup, 4-6 tablespoons arrowroot powder, & 2 teaspoons vanilla until smooth and creamy. Chill for 15- 20 minutes.

CHOCOLATE PUDDING CAKE WITH WHIPPED CREAM AND FRESH BERRIES

Chocolate Pudding Cake

Cinnamon "Cookie" Layer
I call these cookies, but they are really more like flat, thin, cake layers.

Ingredients:
1 cup almond flour
1 cup finely ground pecans
Sprinkle of cinnamon
1 tablespoon grape seed oil
¼ cup honey
1 teaspoon vanilla extract
2 eggs

Combine ingredients, stir well and form dough into 3 balls. This is a sticky dough. You can sprinkle a little gluten free flour on them to help with the stickiness. Place between two pieces of parchment paper and roll out one ball at a time. Peel the top layer of parchment paper away and place the parchment paper with rolled out dough on a cookie sheet. Poke some holes in the dough with a fork. You can cut the edges to make a circle or square or leave them more amorphous in shape. Bake at 350° for 10-12 minutes. Cool on a rack. Once cooled and set, peel away parchment paper.

Memories
My mom would whip this up quick if we got word that unexpected company was on the way. Only she made it with graham crackers. Since they aren't gluten free, I created the cookie layer out of nuts instead.

Alchemy Tips:
I like rolling the dough out into amoeba-like forms. I think it adds character to have irregular shapes, but you can trim the edges with a knife to make a square and give it clean edges.

To Make the Cake, layer cookie and chocolate pudding on page 77 with your bottom layer as cookie and your top layer pudding. Chill in refrigerator for 1-2 hours. Top with whipped cream page 77 and berries.

CHOCOLATE PUDDING TOPPED
WITH FRESH FRUIT & COCONUT

Chocolate Pudding

Ingredients:
1/3 cup raw cacao
1/3 cup organic corn starch or tapioca starch
Pinch of sea salt
3 cups whole milk or dairy-free milk of your choice*
2 teaspoons vanilla extract
¾ cup sugar or coconut palm sugar

Combine dry ingredients in a sauce pan. Add in liquid ingredients except vanilla. Whisk to eliminate any lumps. Cook over medium heat, stirring constantly. Continue to stir constantly for about 3 minutes until the mixture becomes a thick velvety texture. If you stop stirring earlier, the mixture will get lumpy. Remove from heat and stir in vanilla.

Whipped Cream
8 oz heavy cream
1-2 tablespoons maple syrup or coconut nectar
1 teaspoon vanilla extract

Place all of the ingredients in a chilled mixing bowl. Begin beating on low speed and gradually increase the speed as the cream thickens. Stop periodically to test for stiff peaks that stand on their own, but be careful not to over beat or you will have butter.

Alchemy Tips:
You can replace the cornstarch with arrowroot powder. However, it can be a little tricky to work with, so I prefer tapioca as a cornstarch alternative.

If you use arrowroot, stop stirring and remove from heat once the pudding thickens. If you continue stirring, the pudding may thin out again.

*Rice milk and soy milk, due to their low fat content, may need more starch to thicken. Add 1 tablespoon at a time until desired thickness is achieved.

BONBONS WITH FROZEN
RASPBERRIES

Frozen Coconut Cream Bonbons

This recipe was inspired by the ice cream bonbons that were popular during my teen years, as well as the "nice cream" recipes that are popping up all over the internet. I've been playing around with making my own dairy and dairy-free ice cream for a few years, but no matter what I do, once the ice cream goes into the freezer for more than an hour, it freezes into a hard block and needs time to thaw before scooping. Since I prefer immediate gratification, I decided that it was easier to put spoonfuls on a cookie tray and freeze them in bite size pieces.

Cool & Creamy

Alchemy Tips: Chill your beater before whipping your cream. If your cream isn't thickening, you can add 1-2 tablespoons of arrowroot powder, adding 1 tablespoon at a time.

Vanilla version Ingredients:
1 can coconut cream
1 1/2 tablespoons vanilla extract
2 tablespoons pure maple syrup

Chocolate version:
Add 2-3 tablespoons raw cacao powder plus another tablespoon maple syrup to the vanilla recipe.

Make an "Almond Joy" version:
Add a handful of shredded coconut and almonds to the vanilla or chocolate version.

Put the coconut cream in the refrigerator for several hours, so the milk and cream separate. Once chilled, pour off the milk and use in a smoothie or store in a glass jar in the refrigerator. Put the cream in the mixing bowl with the other ingredients. Start mixer on low and slowly increase until cream thickens into a whipped cream consistency. I've noticed that some brands thicken more quickly than others. Continue with instructions on page 81.

ALMOND JOY BONBON

Bonbons and Frosting All-In-One Recipe

To make bonbons put little spoonfuls of the cream onto a wax paper lined chilled cookie sheet and put in the freezer to chill for about 10 minutes. Then pour a spoonful of the chocolate coating recipe on each frozen spoonful and place back into the freezer to chill. If not eating right away, store in a covered container in freezer. Use the chocolate recipe below to make a chocolate coating.

Chocolate coating:
2 tablespoons coconut oil
1 tablespoon raw cacao
2 tablespoons pure maple syrup
¼ teaspoon vanilla extract

Create a double boiler by putting water in one pot and putting another pot containing coconut oil and cacao top of it. Over medium-low heat, whisk the oil and cacao until the oil is completely melted and there are no cacao lumps. Turn off the heat and whisk in the vanilla and maple syrup. Then spoon over frozen coconut cream and refreeze.

Versatility

Alchemy Tips: You can also spoon this recipe into dishes to eat as a chocolate mousse-like dessert or use as frosting on cakes and cupcakes.

As a frosting: If using as a frosting, for best results, frost just before eating, or store in the refrigerator between frosting and eating.

Chocolate Coating Shortcut: Melt ¼ cup chocolate chips plus 1 tablespoon coconut oil in a double boiler.

CASHEW CREAM WITH
FROZEN BERRIES

Cashew Cream With Berries

Ingredients:
1 cup raw, unsalted cashews (soaked in water over night)
1 1/2 tablespoons pure organic maple syrup or coconut nectar
1 1/2 tablespoons almond or coconut milk
1 1/2 tablespoons vanilla extract
1-2 cloves
Dash of cinnamon
Dash of cardamom
Bowl full of your favorite berries

Soak a cup of raw, unsalted cashews overnight in a bowl of water. Drain off the water before preparing the cashew cream.

Put all of the ingredients in a food processor, Vitamix, or blender and blend until it becomes a creamy consistency. The consistency will be similar to almond butter but a little looser.

Add more or less cinnamon and cardamom to taste.

Balance

Alchemy Tips:
Use as a protein-packed topping on top of berries.

I think raspberries and strawberries go best with this cream.

The tart acidity of the berries pairs perfectly with the rich, creaminess of the cashew cream.

PECAN PIE Á LA MODE

Pecan Apple Pie

Most pecan pies are loaded not only with tons of sugar, but also high fructose corn syrup. Not this one though.

Crust Ingredients:
1 package Bob's Red Mill Gluten-free Pie Crust
12 tablespoons butter or non-dairy shortening
4-6 tablespoons water

Filling Ingredients:
4 medium sized apples
3 large eggs
1 tablespoon vanilla
½ teaspoon cinnamon + some for sprinkling
¼ cup maple syrup
2 tablespoons palm sugar or brown sugar
3 tablespoons butter or coconut oil
¼ cup coarsely ground pecans
1 cup chopped pecans or pecan halves

Prepare the pie crust according to package directions, roll out the dough and place it in the pie dish. Preheat the oven to 350°. Poke holes with a fork in the bottom of the crust. Cut apple slices and arrange them in the pie dish and sprinkle cinnamon on them. Melt the butter and let it cool slightly. Crack the eggs into a bowl, add vanilla, cinnamon, maple syrup, melted butter and sugar. Whisk until well combined. Fold in the pecans and pour over the apples in the pie dish. Bake at 350° for about 50 minutes.

Cool on a rack.

If you like, serve with coconut cream, whipped cream or your favorite ice cream.

Two Classic Pies Made Into One

Alchemy Tips: Bob's gives you enough dough for a covered pie. This is an uncovered pie, so you can freeze half for another time or make two pies by doubling the filling ingredients.

If your dough crumbles while rolling it out, you can press it into the bottom and sides of the pie dish.

BANANA TEA

Banana Tea

I love being able to use all of the parts of our food in some way. When I first heard the idea of banana tea, I was skeptical, but it really is delicious. I've modified Dr. Breus version by using only the peel and adding spices, milk and honey.

Ingredients:
1 organic banana peel-washed
3 cups water
Your favorite milk*
3-4 cloves
1 cinnamon stick
Dash of ground nutmeg or cardamom
Teaspoon raw honey

Bring the peel, water, cloves and cinnamon to a boil on the stove and boil on medium heat for approximately 10 minutes to make a tea. Pour the tea into a mug and add milk, a dash of nutmeg or cardamom and honey. Enjoy!

This tea can be served hot or cold. I like hot best, especially when using as a sleep aid.

In addition to the sleep benefits of magnesium, cinnamon is warming to the body which may help one to relax. The cloves and nutmeg are also known to help promote sleep.

*I like to use an almond-coconut blend.

Evening Elixir

This recipe was inspired by Michael Breus, PhD., The Sleep Doctor. He recommends making a tea by boiling a banana and its peel in water to his patients who have difficulty sleeping.

The peel is said to have 3 times the amount of magnesium as the fruit. When it is boiled in the water, the magnesium is released into the tea along with a yummy banana flavor.

EUROPEAN STYLE DUMPLINGS

European Style Dumplings

Ingredients:
2 large eggs
½ cup brown rice flour
¼ cup potato flour
¼ cup tapioca flour + 1 tablespoon
½ cup milk or soup broth
2 tablespoons Parmesan/Romano cheese
1 teaspoon garlic powder
Salt & pepper to taste
½ to 1 teaspoon fresh chopped rosemary

Combine the ingredients until well-incorporated and free of lumps. The dough should be thick.

Drop a spoonful at a time into a pot of boiling water or broth. The dough will drop to the bottom of the pot, and will then rise to the top as it cooks.

Remove dumplings one at a time and drain in a colander, or on a piece of parchment paper, as they continue to set.

Transfer to a serving dish and top with butter, salt and pepper, or other favorite seasonings or sauces. Feel free to add more seasoning to your liking.

Comfort Food

These dumplings are a great cool weather comfort food, and pair nicely with stews and sauces.

Alchemy Tips:

To Make a dairy- free versions: Use a soup broth in place of milk.

For extra flavor, they can also be cooked in soup broth instead of water.

STUFFING

Stuffing

Ingredients:
5 cups Gluten Free bread*
2 tablespoons olive oil, butter or bacon fat
1 handful chopped fresh parsley
1 large onion, chopped
2 stalks celery, chopped
1 large carrot chopped
1 cup GF chicken, turkey or vegetable stock (plus a little extra)
1 cup GF sausage (optional)
1 teaspoon poultry seasoning**

Put bread cubes and parsley in a mixing bowl. In a sauté pan, heat oil & add onion, carrots, celery, and sausage. Sauté until sausage is cooked & veggies have a glazed look. Add stock and poultry seasoning and bring to a simmer. Pour stock mixture over the bread cubes and stir. Let sit for a couple of minutes and fluff with a fork. Add salt & pepper to taste. Sprinkle in a little more soup stock if stuffing is too dry.

Holiday Favorite

Alchemy Tips:

For best results, don't put the stuffing inside the bird just make as directed.

Stuffing it into the bird while it cooks, will over cook the gluten free bread which doesn't stand up well to over cooking.

Vegetarian Stuffing: Use vegetable stock and omit the sausage.

Yields: about 10- ½ cup servings.

*****Bread cubes:** Cut your favorite bread into cubes and dry in the oven on the lowest heat or use a premade bread cube. I like using the Glutino brand stuffing bread cubes.

******Seasoning:** Do a seasoning taste test. If you like more flavor, sprinkle in some more poultry seasoning, or for a real zesty stuffing, try a dash of cayenne pepper added to the soup broth.

MY STORY

I felt like I was dying. About 15 years ago, I was working as a Counselor and Program Director with court ordered clients. Working with the court system can be a high drama, high stress, contentious experience, but I loved it. During this time, I started having serious health problems. I was experiencing digestive distress, including a pain on the right side of my abdomen. I was exhausted all of the time. I had migraines almost daily. My bones and joints ached deep down. The pain was constant and I could even feel the pain in my sleep. I often thought to myself, there must be something seriously wrong with me. At the time, I was only in my mid-thirties and my parents, who were in their seventies, were energetic and full of life. With the exception of my husband who got to hear me complain, and my mother, who noticed that I wasn't smiling anymore, no one really knew how much I was suffering, because I dragged myself through the day doing whatever needed to get done.

I knew something needed to change, if I were to make it into my seventies and beyond. My sister and cousin were already diagnosed with celiac disease, and suggested that I stop eating gluten. Although I was feeling lousy, I was not ready to give up pizza, pasta and bread. I was in complete denial. I cut back on my work hours so that I was only working 40 hours a week. I decided to take up yoga, eat more fruits and vegetables and started walking daily. I also went to see a gastroenterologist and had a full work up of tests that spanned over about six to eight months. To my surprise, all of my tests were negative. This was great news! I wasn't dying, but why was I feeling so lousy all of the time?

I questioned how my tests could be negative, when I had pain in my gut every time I ate something. The doctor reassured me that he believed I had real pain, but that he just wasn't smart enough to figure it out yet. Yes, those were his actual words. Although I appreciated his honesty, I was feeling lost and confused. He told me to watch what I ate and come back in three to four months. I said, "But I have pain every time I eat. Am I just supposed to be in pain for the next three to four months? And what does it mean, actually, to watch what I eat?" At that point, he gave me a pain killer.

As he handed the prescription to me, he winked and said that the pain killer would also help with my migraines. I left that appointment feeling furious. I decided that if he wasn't going to be smart enough to figure things out, I would. That was a pivotal point in my healing journey.

I did not go back to that doctor and I did not fill the prescription for the pain killers. I researched my symptoms and what nutritionists and holistic health providers were recommending to help heal the body. I started taking a probiotic and digestive enzymes. I switched from whole wheat bread, which I thought was nutritious for me, to sprouted bread. I did a sugar cleanse and took some other supplements.

At that point, I was feeling 75% better, but I still had an ache in the right side of my abdomen that would come a few minutes into my meal and I still had some stiffness and inflammation in my joints. I knew the next step would be to go to a holistic practitioner in person, but I also knew that I didn't want to, because I would probably have to give up some of my favorite foods.

I finally gave in and chose my health. I found a lovely holistic practitioner whose approach to healthy eating came from a place of intuition, love and abundance rather than discipline and deprivation. She listened patiently to my story and my frustrations. She introduced me to quinoa and told me that I didn't need to cut coffee and sugar completely out of my diet, but that it would be to my benefit to work on cutting back on them. She suggested that although I tested negative for celiac disease, that I could still have a sensitivity to wheat and gluten, especially since it runs in my family. I left the hour long appointment feeling hopeful. I had suggestions and recipes in hand and the message to make small changes and experiment over the next two weeks until we met again.

In the past, when I had tried cutting out wheat and gluten, I did so for about a day or two which isn't enough time for the body to heal enough to feel a difference. This time, I decided that I would take things seriously and read every label. I tried the recipes from the holistic doctor and didn't eat even a crumb of wheat or gluten. Within three days, I noticed a huge difference and decided to continue on. I decided that I was giving up wheat and gluten. However, every now and then, I would "treat and cheat" with pizza and Dunkin Donuts. Each time I cheated, my symptoms were worse than the time before, and eventually, I no longer had a desire to cheat. Feeling healthy felt so good and feeling lousy felt so horrible.

My healing journey continued for the next few years which included helping my friends and family understand that I wasn't cutting out wheat and gluten because it was a diet choice or fad. I was doing it to not feel sick and to be healthy. Once I cut out wheat and gluten for good, I had much more energy. My mood improved. My gut stopped hurting and my bones and joints stopped hurting as well. Friends and family would comment that I must have discipline and willpower. The truth is, you don't need discipline and willpower once you choose loving yourself and feeling good over all other things.

There is something that happens when we take charge of our own healing. It brings healing to the Spirit as well as the body. I hear from so many people about how the current health care system has a lack of understanding about how the foods we eat impact our health, as well as a lack of compassion for the psychological impact and loss associated with a diagnosis of a food sensitivity or Celiac Disease. I've even had clients tell me that when they bring up food and nutrition, their doctor, responds that they can look into it, if they want, but it will probably have little impact. In my mind, this is an injustice. Eventually, the world will wake up and realize once again that we are what we eat and as Hippocrates said so long ago, "Let food be thy medicine, and medicine be thy food."

I'm sharing this story to let you know that you can feel better, too. If you've been making changes to your food and lifestyle and you're still not felling your best, don't give up. Keep seeking and experimenting with different solutions and be open to alternative sources of healing. I wish you the best along your healing journey and I would love to hear from you. You can connect with me at www.jbenderwellness.com.

Resources

I'm not paid to endorse any particular brands, but these are my favorites and things that I use most often and things that I think could be helpful for you.

Essential Oils: For the essential oils used in these recipes, go to ***Young Living Essential Oils*** - www.youngliving.com
I am a member of Young Living Oils, because I love and believe in their products. If you decide to become a member and need a referral number, mine is #1829926. I'd also be happy to answer any questions you might have. You can connect with me at www.jbenderwellness.com.

Gluten Free Flour Resources:
Bob's Red Mill www.bobsredmill.com
Arrowhead Mills www.arrowheadmills.com
King Arthur Flour www.kingarthurflour.com
Nut.com www.nuts.com

Aluminum Free Baking Powder Brands:
Rumford www.clabbergirl.com
Bob's Red Mill www.bobsredmill.com
Argo www.argostarch.com

Natural Sweeteners:
Sweet Leaf Stevia www.sweetleaf.com
Organic Zing Stevia www.zingstevia.com
Coconut Nectar www.coconutsecret.com

Natural Food Dyes and Sprinkles:
Color Garden www.colorgarden.net
India Tree www.Indiatree.com

Incredi-Whip www.drshicashealthysurprises.com

Tulsi Tea www.organicindia.com

Gluten-free, Dairy-free, Nut-free Chocolate Chips
www.enjoylifefoods.com

Gluten-free Bread Cubes www.glutino.com

For just about all of your bake ware and ingredient needs-
www.Amazon.com

Gadgets, Appliances and Apps:
Nima Food Testing Sensor and the Nima App. You can now test to see if the food you're eating contains gluten using this small handheld device. For more information, go to www.nimasensor.com

High Speed Blenders
I have both a Vitamix and a Ninja. I love them both, but I have to say that I do use my Ninja more. It has a variety of containers and blades. Both brands have a variety of price points. If you want to compare them, here are their websites.
www.vitamix.com
www.ninjakitchen.com

Notes